SCHOLASTIC

Phonics Activities

TO MEET THE

Common Core

BY MARGARET P. SHORTER

NEW YORK ● TORONTO ● LONDON ● AUCKLAND ● SYDNEY
MEXICO CITY ● NEW DELHI ● HONG KONG ● BUENOS AIRES

Teaching Resources

Written by Margaret P. Shorter
Edited by Immacula A. Rhodes
Cover design by Scott Davis
Interior design by Kathy Massaro
Interior illustrations by Teresa Anderko, Maxie Chambliss, Rusty Fletcher, and Rush Linstromberg

ISBN 978-0-545-53834-3

1 2 3 4 5 6 7 8 9 10   40   21 20 19 18 17 16 15 14

Contents

○ ◉ ○

Phonics Activities

About This Book

○ ◉ ○

*P*honics Activities to Meet the Common Core offers fun, engaging ways to motivate children of all learning styles and help them master essential phonics skills. In addition, the 15 activities in this book are designed to meet the Language Arts standards identified by the Common Core State Standards Initiative in Foundational Skills for Reading. (See page 6 for more information.)

Research shows that a strong foundation in phonics is an important component in building reading confidence and fluency. In his book *Phonics From* A *to* Z: *A Practical Guide, 2ⁿᵈ Edition* (Scholastic, 2006), reading specialist Wiley Blevins notes that the faster children can decode words, the more words they recognize by sight, the more time and energy they have to devote to the meaning of the text (Freeman and Calfee, 1984; LaBerge and Samuels, 1974). Blevins cites Cunningham's (1995) observation that the brain works as a "pattern detector." Since blends, digraphs, word families, and many vowel sounds contain reliable sound-spelling patterns, learning to recognize their common patterns increases children's sight word vocabulary. The phonics activities in this resource give children the opportunity to practice common sound-spelling relationships and develop automaticity in word recognition, which in turn helps build their reading fluency and comprehension.

Quick and easy to prepare, these activities can be used for instruction with the whole class, small groups, student pairs, or individuals. They are also ideal for independent work, centers, practice with partners, and homework. Multisensory features provide visual, auditory, and tactile reinforcement to help children really learn the key phonics skills they need to succeed in reading. And best of all, the activities are ideal for children of all learning styles, RTI students, and second-language learners.

Phonics Activities to Meet the Common Core © 2014 by Scholastic Teaching Resources

What's Inside

Each activity in this resource targets a specific phonics skill. To use, simply decide on the skill you want to teach, check the Contents on page 3 to locate the corresponding activity, then gather the materials and follow the directions to prepare it. Here's what you'll find in the lessons:

* an introductory activity that provides a suggestion for introducing the phonics skill and related activity

* a list of materials—including reproducible patterns—needed to prepare the activity

* easy, step-by-step directions that tell how to prepare and use the activity

* an extension activity designed to reinforce children's skills and interest

* tips for preparing or using the activity

Helpful Tips

* Store the components for each phonics activity in a large, resealable plastic bag. Label the bag with the name of the activity.

* Place each individual set of cards in separate resealable sandwich bags to keep the cards sorted.

* Gather the materials needed to make the activities in advance. Most use basic classroom supplies.

* Familiarize yourself with the activities and their use before introducing them to the class.

* Demonstrate how to complete the activities before having children use them independently.

* Feel free to customize or adapt the activities to expand the scope of the skills to be practiced. For example, you might prepare additional puzzles in Vowel Pair Puzzles to teach words spelled with a particular vowel pair, such as *oa*.

Connections to the Common Core State Standards

The Common Core State Standards Initiative (CCSSI) has outlined learning expectations in English Language Arts for students at different grade levels. The activities in this book align with the following Foundational Skills for Reading for students in grades K–2. For more information, visit the CCSSI Web site at www.corestandards.org.

Phonological Awareness

- RF.K.2, RF.1.2. Demonstrate understanding of spoken words, syllables, and sounds (phonemes).
- RF.K.2a. Recognize and produce rhyming words.
- RF.K.2b. Count, pronounce, blend, and segment syllables in spoken words.
- RF.K.2c. Blend and segment onsets and rimes of single-syllable spoken words.
- RF.K.2d. Isolate and pronounce the initial, medial vowel, and final sounds (phonemes) in three-phoneme (consonant-vowel-consonant or CVC) words.
- RF.K.2e. Add or substitute individual sounds (phonemes) in simple, one-syllable words to make new words.
- RF.1.2a. Distinguish long from short vowel sounds in spoken single-syllable words.
- RF.1.2b. Orally produce single-syllable words by blending sounds (phonemes), including consonant blends.
- RF.1.2c. Isolate and pronounce initial, medial vowel, and final sounds (phonemes) in spoken single-syllable words.
- RF.1.2d. Segment spoken single-syllable words into their complete sequence of individual sounds (phonemes).

Phonics and Word Recognition

- RF.K.3, RF.1.3, RF.2.3. Know and apply grade-level phonics and word analysis skills in decoding words.
- RF.K.3a. Demonstrate basic knowledge of one-to-one letter-sound correspondences by producing the primary sound or many of the most frequent sounds for each consonant.
- RF.K.3b. Associate the long and short sounds with the common spellings (graphemes) for the five major vowels.
- RF.K.3c. Read common high-frequency words by sight (e.g., *the, of, to, you, she, my, is, are, do, does*).
- RF.K.3d. Distinguish between similarly spelled words by identifying the sounds of the letters that differ.
- RF.1.3a. Know the spelling-sound correspondences for common consonant digraphs.
- RF.1.3b. Decode regularly spelled one-syllable words.
- RF.1.3c. Know final -e and common vowel team conventions for representing long vowel sounds.
- RF.1.3d. Use knowledge that every syllable must have a vowel sound to determine the number of syllables in a printed word.
- RF.1.3e. Decode two-syllable words following basic patterns by breaking the words into syllables.
- RF.1.3g. Recognize and read grade-appropriate irregularly spelled words.
- RF.2.3a. Distinguish long and short vowels when reading regularly spelled one-syllable words.
- RF.2.3b. Know the spelling-sound correspondences for additional common vowel teams.
- RF.2.3c. Decode regularly spelled two-syllable words with long vowels.
- RF.2.3d. Decode words with common prefixes and suffixes.
- RF.2.3e. Identify words with inconsistent but common spelling-sound correspondences.
- RF.2.3f. Recognize and read grade-appropriate irregularly spelled words.

Fluency

- RF.K.4. Read emergent-reader texts with purpose and understanding.
- RF.1.4, RF.2.4. Read with sufficient accuracy and fluency to support comprehension.
- RF.1.4a, RF.2.4a. Read on-level text with purpose and understanding.
- RF.1.4c, RF.2.4c. Use context to confirm or self-correct word recognition and understanding, rereading as necessary.

Initial Consonant Catch

This cast of fishing bears provides lots of opportunities for children to catch on to the concept of letter-sound associations.

Introduce the Concept

Show each picture card and have children say its name. Then have them sound out only the beginning sound of the word and identify the letter that represents that sound. If desired, write the word on the board to help reinforce the letter-sound connection. Finally, invite children to finger-write the letter in the air while saying the sound it makes.

Preparing and Using the Activity

1. Color and cut out the bear and fish cards.

2. Laminate the cards for durability.

3. Review the letter on each bear.

4. To use, have children name the picture on each fish. They then identify its beginning sound and the letter for that sound.

5. Ask children to find the bear labeled with the matching letter and place the fish on that card.

Extend the Activity

To reinforce additional initial consonants (or vowels), make a copy of the blank bear and fish card for each new letter you want to feature. Write each new letter on a bear and glue a picture that corresponds to the letter on a fish. Laminate, if desired.

Materials

- bear cards (pages 8–11)
- fish cards (page 12)
- crayons
- scissors

✳ ✦ Tip ✦ ✳

Give children a copy of the activity cards to color and cut out. Have them glue each fish to the matching bear card. Then encourage children to take their cards home to find other words that begin with the same sound.

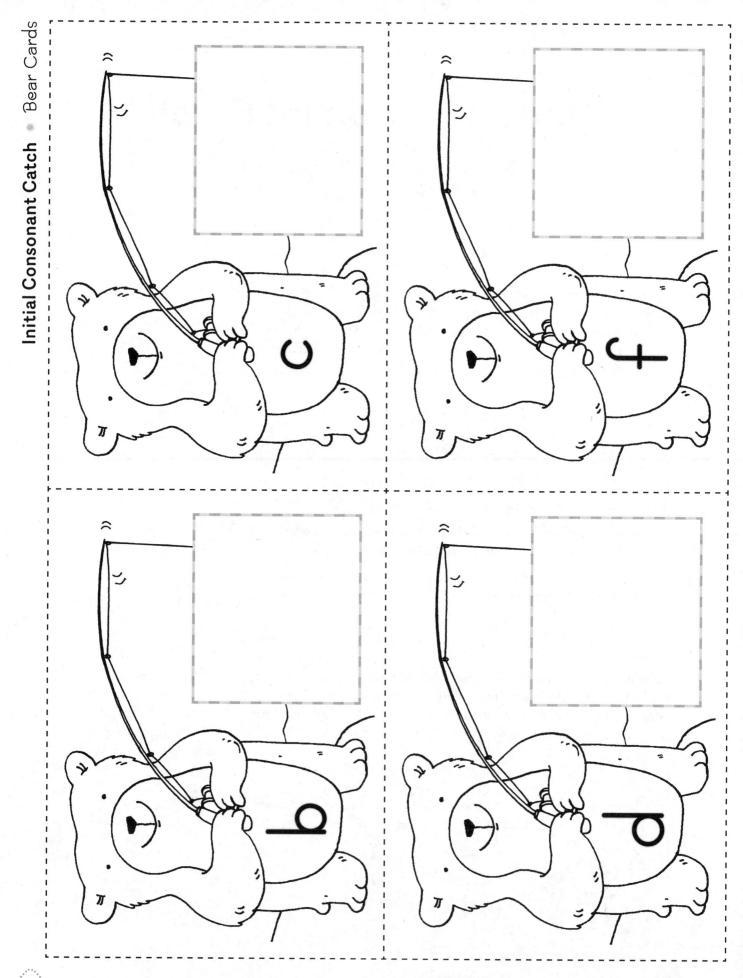

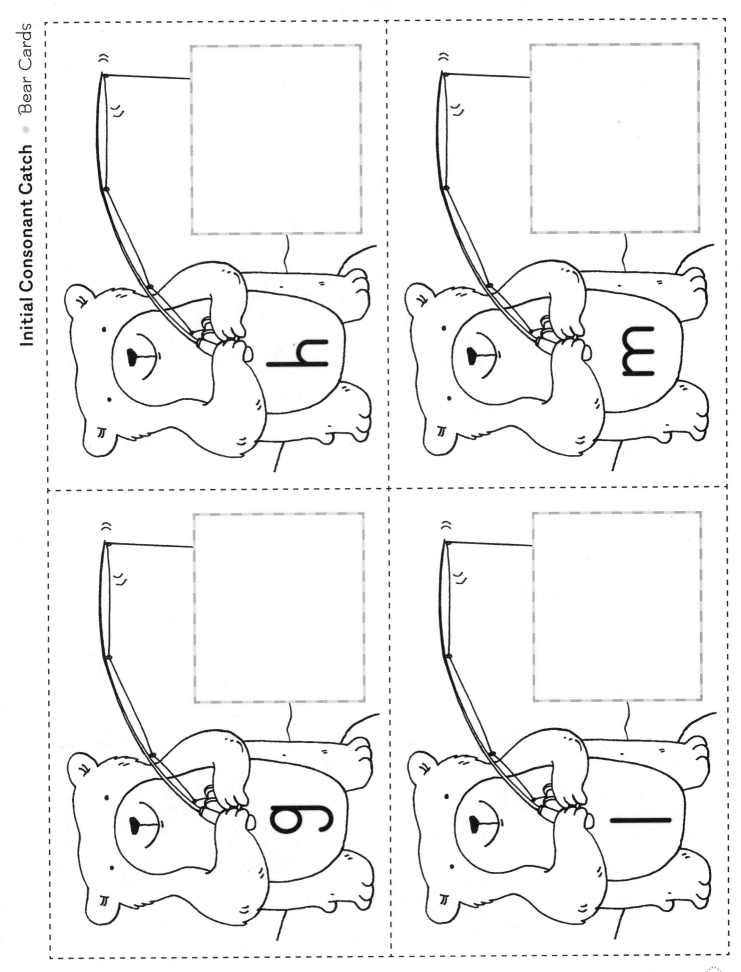

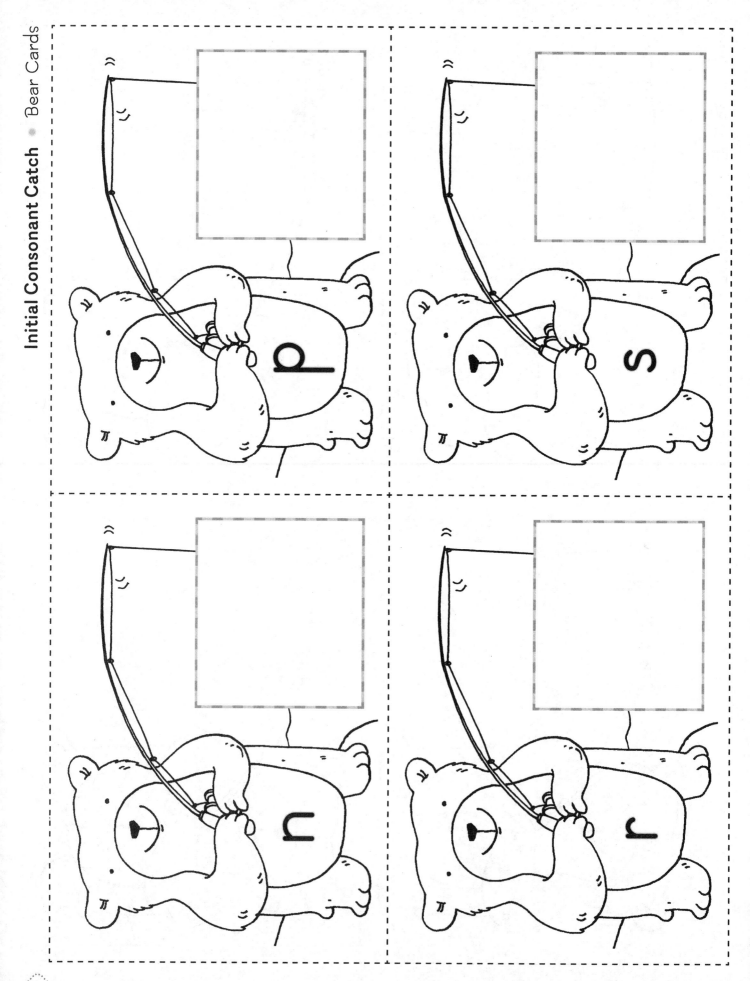

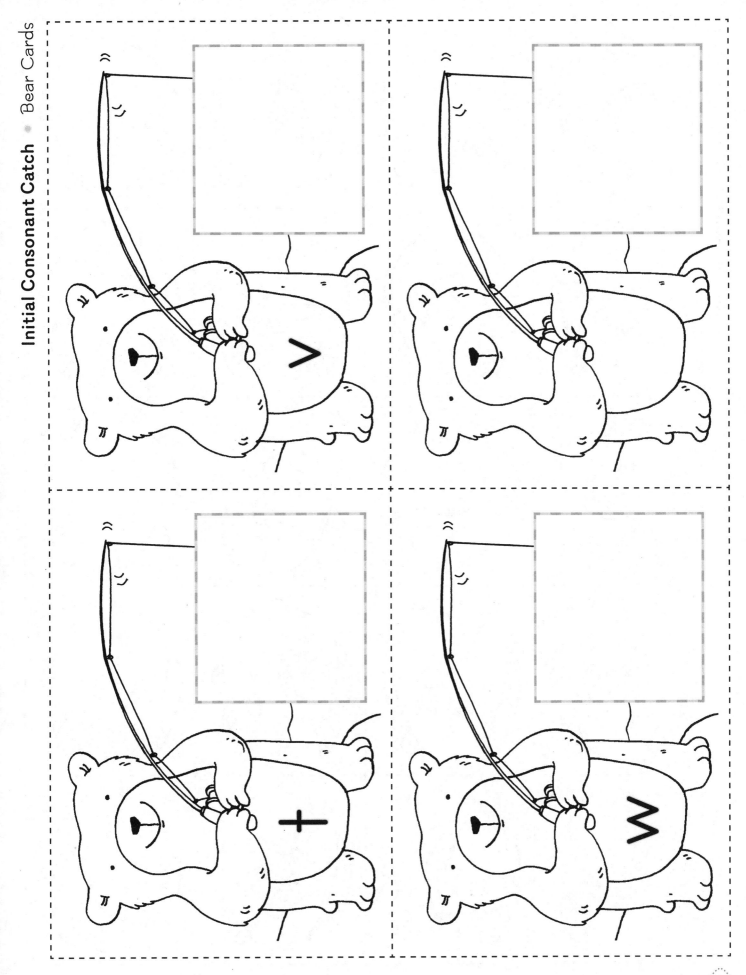

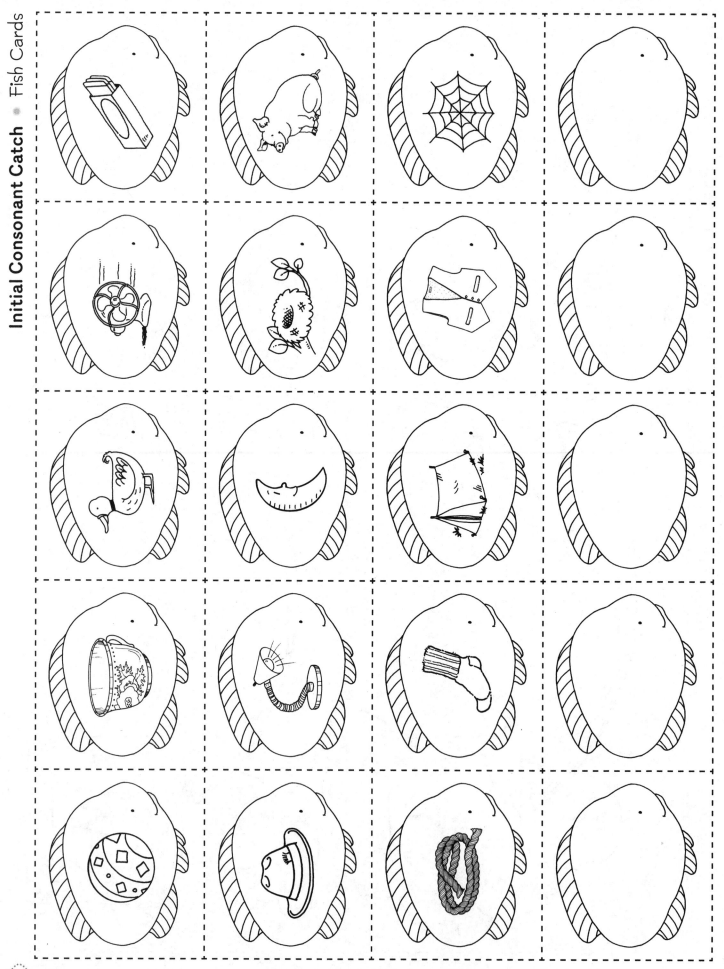

Phonics Activities to Meet the Common Core © 2014 by Scholastic Teaching Resources

Build-a-Word Pull-Throughs

These clever pull-throughs let children make dozens of CVC words as they practice letter-sound associations in the initial and final position.

Introduce the Concept

Draw two boxes at the top of the board, one at the top left and the other at the top right. Write the letters *b, f, p,* and *w* in the box on the left and *d, g, n* and *t* in the box on the right. In the space just below and between the boxes, write a vowel, such as *i*. Then challenge children to make new words with the vowel, using letters from the left box for the beginning letters and those from the right box for final letters (for example, *bid, fit, pig,* and *win*). How many new words can they come up with? As they work, encourage children to sound out the initial and final consonants slowly and clearly.

Preparing and Using the Activity

1. Color and cut out the pull-through shape of your choice. Also, cut out a copy of the initial and final letter strips. (Note that there are three initial letter strips.)

2. Laminate the pull-through shapes and letter strips for durability.

3. Use the craft knife to cut the two slits on each side of the vowel on the pull-through shapes.

4. Thread an initial consonant letter strip through the slits on the left. (Match the circle symbols.) Then thread the final consonant letter strip through the slits on the right. (These have a triangle symbol.)

5. Have children pull each strip through the slits so that only one letter appears both before and after the vowel. Do the three letters together make a word? If so, they write the word on a sheet of paper.

6. Have children pull the strips to make as many words as possible.

Extend the Activity

To further reinforce letter-sound association skills, have children group their words by beginning letters (or endings letters). You might also challenge children to group words together that have both the same beginning and ending letters, such as *bat, bet, bit,* and *but.*

Materials

- pull-through shapes (pages 14–18)
- letter strips (page 19)
- crayons
- scissors
- craft knife (for adult use only)
- paper and pencil (for students)

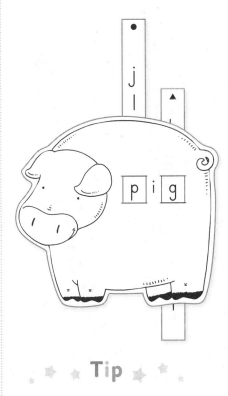

Tip

In addition to teaching initial and final consonant sounds, you can use the pull-throughs to help teach and reinforce the short vowel sound of CVC words.

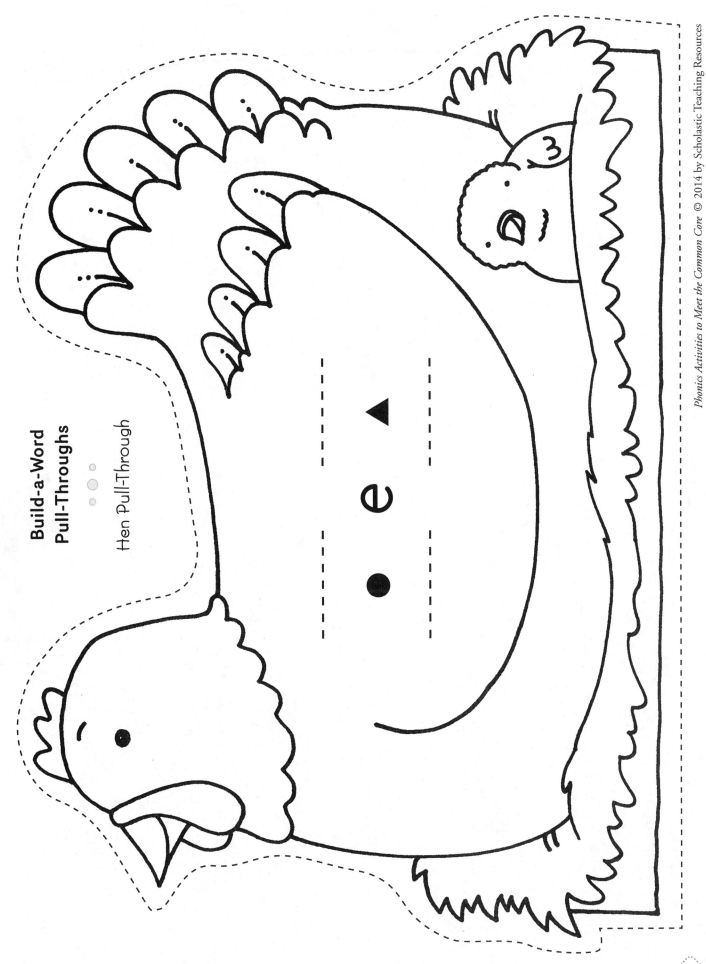

Build-a-Word Pull-Throughs

Hen Pull-Through

e

Phonics Activities to Meet the Common Core © 2014 by Scholastic Teaching Resources

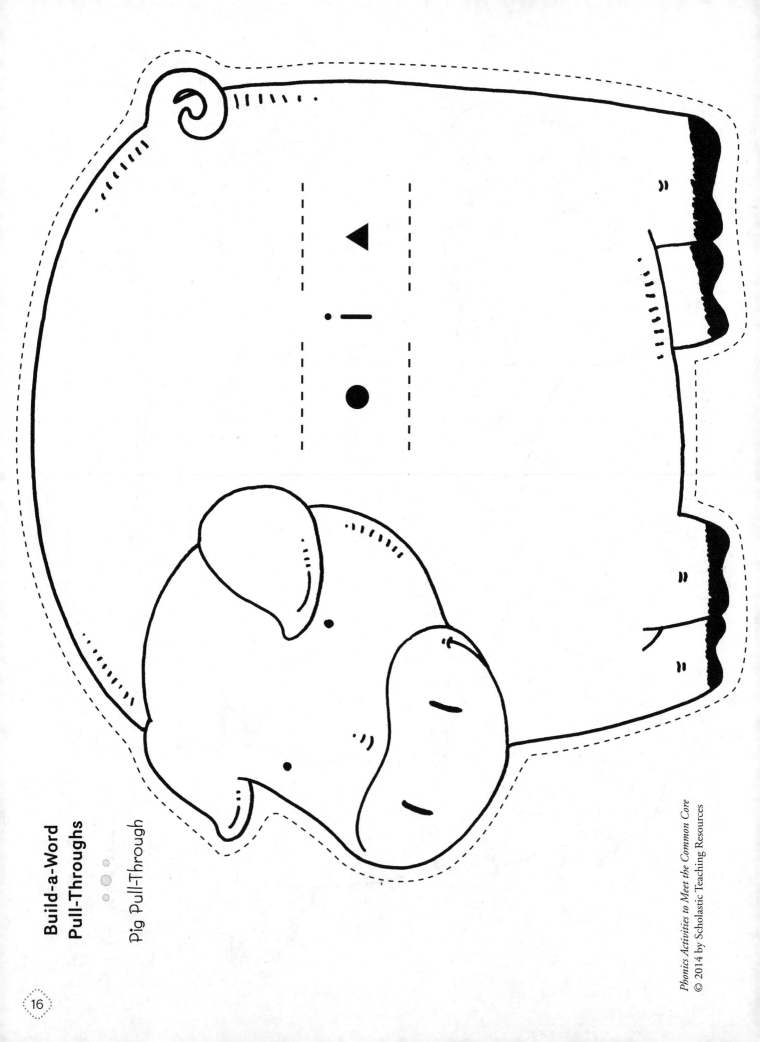

**Build-a-Word
Pull-Throughs**

Pig Pull-Through

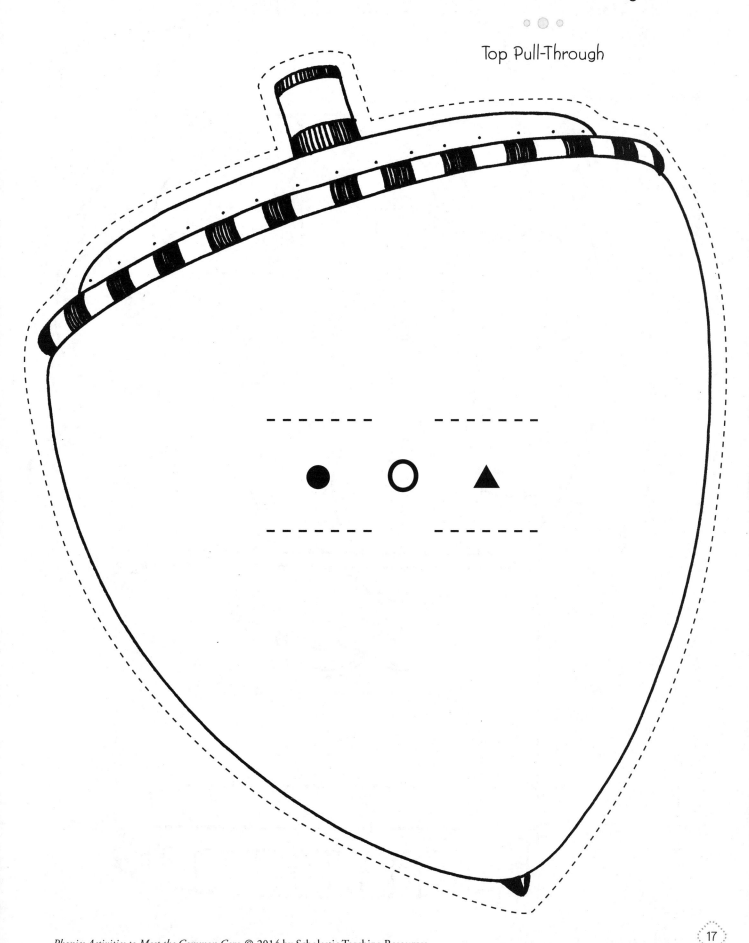

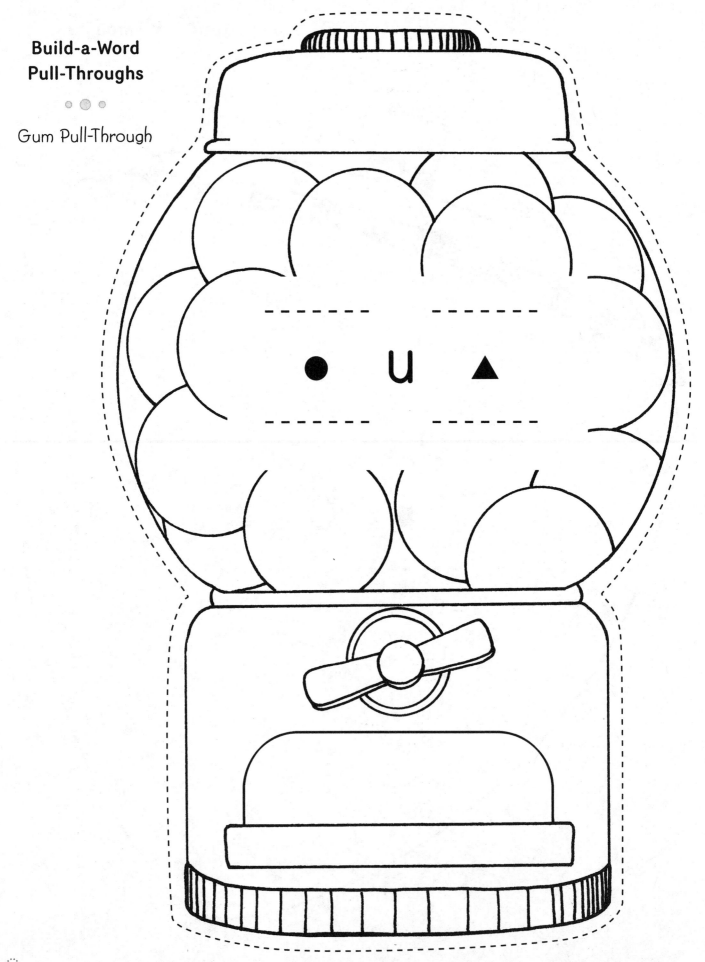

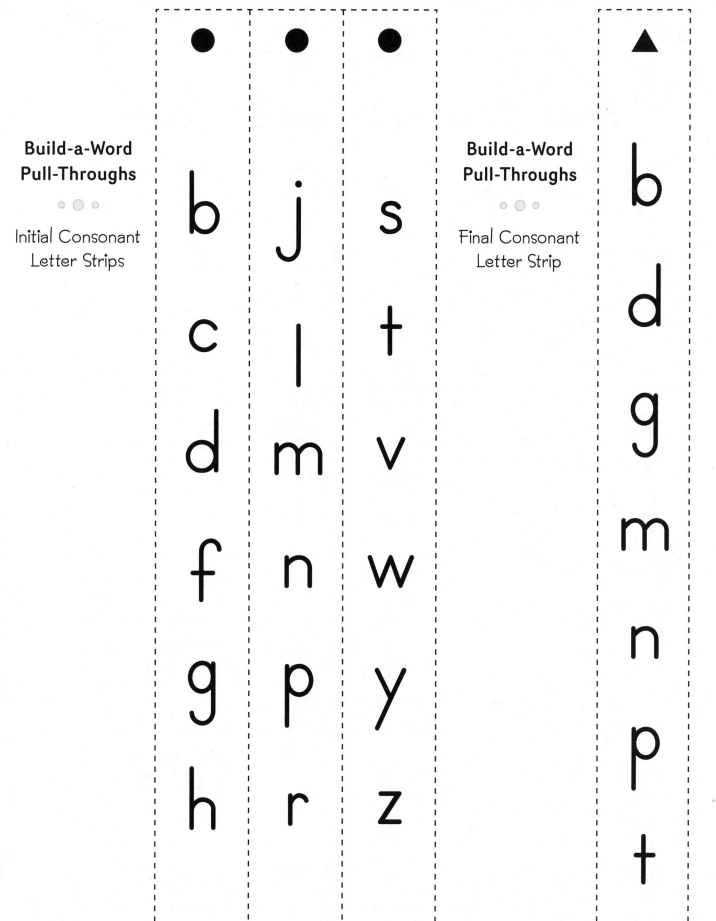

Build-a-Word Pull-Throughs

Initial Consonant Letter Strips

Build-a-Word Pull-Throughs

Final Consonant Letter Strip

b	j	s
c	l	t
d	m	v
f	n	w
g	p	y
h	r	z

b
d
g
m
n
p
t

Short & Long Vowel Boogie

These action-packed ditties provide a fun strategy to help children remember and distinguish between the short and long sound of each vowel.

Materials

- Short-Vowel- and Long-Vowel-Boogie rhymes and word cards (pages 21–22)
- crayons
- scissors

Tip

Give children copies of the rhymes and word cards to take home. Encourage them to teach their friends and family members how to do both boogie dances.

Introduce the Concept

Display the Short-Vowel-Boogie rhyme and picture cards. Say the word on each card and ask children to identify its vowel sound. Is the vowel short or long? Point out that the picture shows an action that represents the word. The actions are as follows: tap (tap foot), step (step forward), kick (kick leg up high), rock (rock side to side), and bump (bump hip to side). Invite children to perform each action, find the word in the rhyme, then point to and sound out the vowel. When finished, repeat for the Long Vowel Boogie. The actions for this rhyme are: shake (shake entire body), freeze (shiver as if cold), slide (slide foot along floor), low (bend forward close to the ground), and mule (kick foot back like a mule).

Preparing and Using the Activity

1. Color and cut out the rhymes and picture cards. Laminate for durability.

2. Display the Short-Vowel-Boogie rhyme and picture cards. Place the cards in the order in which they appear in the rhyme.

3. Pick up the first card (*tap*) and read the word aloud. Then have children read the first line of the rhyme and perform the corresponding action each time they read the word. They are doing the Short Vowel Boogie!

4. Repeat step 3 for each of the remaining four word cards.

5. After doing the Short Vowel Boogie, display the Long-Vowel-Boogie rhyme and picture cards as in step 2. Then repeat steps 3 and 4 to lead children in doing the Long Vowel Boogie.

Extend the Activity

To make the activity more challenging, mix up the order in which you show children the cards. Have them find and read the corresponding line in the rhyme and perform the action. To really keep children on their toes, you might also mix up the word cards for the two boogies.

tap

step

kick

rock

bump

Short Vowel Boogie

Tap /ă/, tap /ă/.

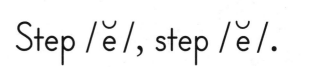

Step /ĕ/, step /ĕ/.

Kick /ĭ/, kick /ĭ/.

Rock /ŏ/, rock /ŏ/.

Bump /ŭ/, bump /ŭ/.

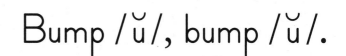

Bump /ŭ/, bump /ŭ/.

Long Vowel Boogie

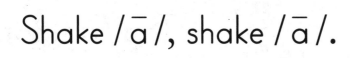

shake

Shake /ā/, shake /ā/.

Freeze /ē/, freeze /ē/.

freeze

Slide /ī/, slide /ī/.

slide

Low /ō/, low /ō/.

low

Mule /ū/, mule /ū/.

Mule /ū/, mule /ū/.

mule

Phonics Activities to Meet the Common Core © 2014 by Scholastic Teaching Resources

Vowel Change Fold-Overs

Children can instantly change short-vowel words to long-vowel words with this fold-over activity.

Introduce the Concept

Write the words *mad*, *bit*, and *hop* on the board. Say each word aloud and ask children to identify its vowel sound. Does the word have a short or long vowel? After establishing that each has a short vowel, explain that the vowel sound in some words can be changed to a long vowel by adding an *e* to the end of the word. Then write an *e* at the end of each word on the board. Say the words with the long vowel sounds (*made*, *bite*, *hope*). Point out that the *e* is silent. Finally, cover the *e* in each word, say the short-vowel word, then uncover the *e* and say the long-vowel word. Repeat several times, inviting children to say the words with you.

Preparing and Using the Activity

1. Color and cut out the fold-over patterns.

2. Cut away the right side of each fold-over. Flip that strip facedown and tape it back in place to create a flap. (For best results, tape both the front and back.) When finished, the short-vowel words and pictures will be face up and the strip with the letter *e* and long-vowel pictures will be face down.

3. Laminate for durability. Then fold the flap back toward the short-vowel words so that the text is faceup. Crease along the taped edge. (Each *e* will line up with a short-vowel word to convert it to a long-vowel word.)

4. To use, have children read each short-vowel word on a fold-over. Then have them fold back the flap and read each new silent-*e* word. Remind children that the *e* converts each short-vowel word to a long-vowel word.

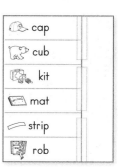

Extend the Activity

Brainstorm with children additional short-vowel words that can be transformed to long-vowel words by adding the silent *e* (for example, *rip/ripe*, *past/paste*, and *mop/mope*). Make a list of both the short- and long-vowel words. Then invite children to illustrate a few of the word pairs. More advanced students might write sentences with word pairs of their choice.

Materials

- fold-over patterns (pages 24–25)
- crayons
- scissors
- clear tape

✷ ✷ Tip ✷ ✷

If desired, cut along the line between each long-vowel picture to create six separate flaps. Then children can convert one short-vowel word at a time by folding back the corresponding flap.

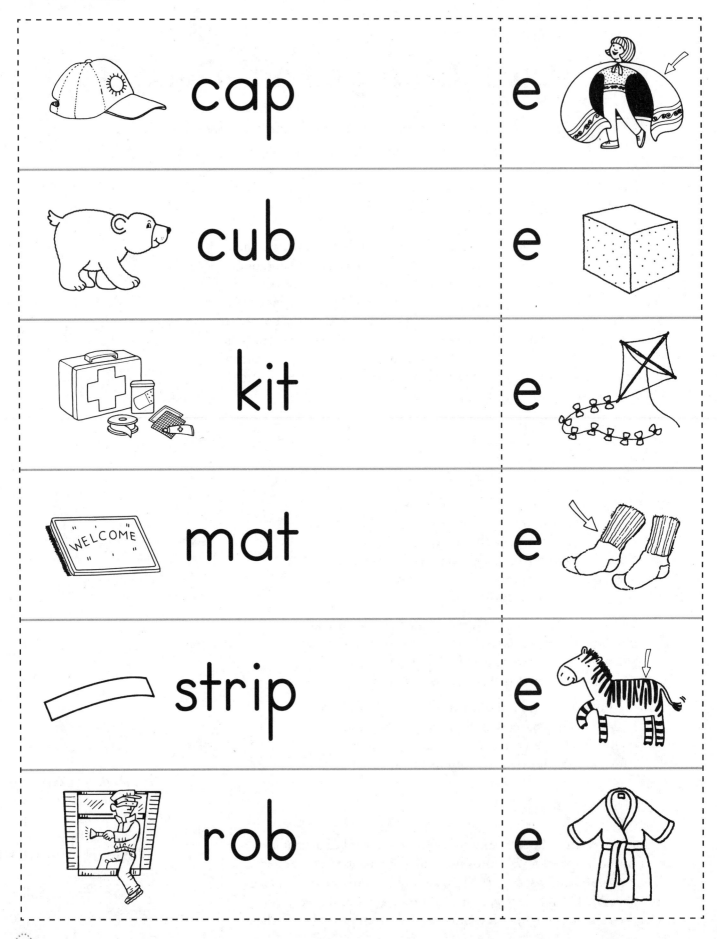

cap   e

cub   e

kit   e

mat   e

strip   e

rob   e

Phonics Activities to Meet the Common Core © 2014 by Scholastic Teaching Resources

can   e

tub   e

glob   e

cut   e

pin   e

van   e

Vowel Pair Puzzles

Help children assemble their understanding of long-vowel digraphs
(vowel pairs) with these unique word puzzles.

Materials

- tagboard puzzle patterns (pages 27–28)
- crayons
- scissors
- paper and pencil (for students)

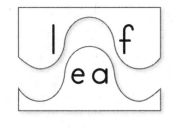

★ Tip ★

You can make your own puzzles to reinforce words with vowel pairs that begin with consonant blends and digraphs, such as *dream, steep, fruit, chain, shine,* and *throat.* Check that the two vowels in each word are always on one puzzle piece and the blend or digraph and final consonant are on the other piece.

Introduce the Concept

Write a few words that contain long-vowel digraphs, such as *boat, leaf,* and *mail,* on the board. Read each word aloud to children, asking them to tell whether the word has a short-vowel or long-vowel sound. After establishing that all the words have long-vowel sounds, point out that each word follows the CVVC spelling pattern. Identify the consonants and vowels in each word. Then explain that in words with this pattern—in which two vowels are paired together between two consonants, the first vowel usually takes the long sound and the second vowel is silent. If desired, explain and share the common phrase, "When two vowels go walking, the first one does the talking." Finally invite children to help you assemble a few of the vowel pair puzzles. Guide them to discover that the consonants are on one piece of each puzzle and the vowels on the other piece.

Preparing and Using the Activity

1. Color and cut out the puzzle patterns. Cut apart each puzzle along the broken line.

2. Laminate the puzzle pieces for durability.

3. To use, have children put the pieces together to make words that contain long-vowel pairs. As they assemble each puzzle, have them spell and say the word.

4. Ask children to write each word they make on a sheet of paper. Invite them to draw pictures for as many of the words as possible.

Extend the Activity

Distribute copies of pages 27–28 and invite children to color and cut out their own set of vowel pair puzzles. Have them assemble their puzzles, then turn over each one and write a new four-letter word that contains a long vowel pair on the back of the pieces. Point out that one piece should be labeled with the consonants and the other with the vowels (as on the reproducible puzzles). Encourage children to share their two-sided puzzles with classmates.

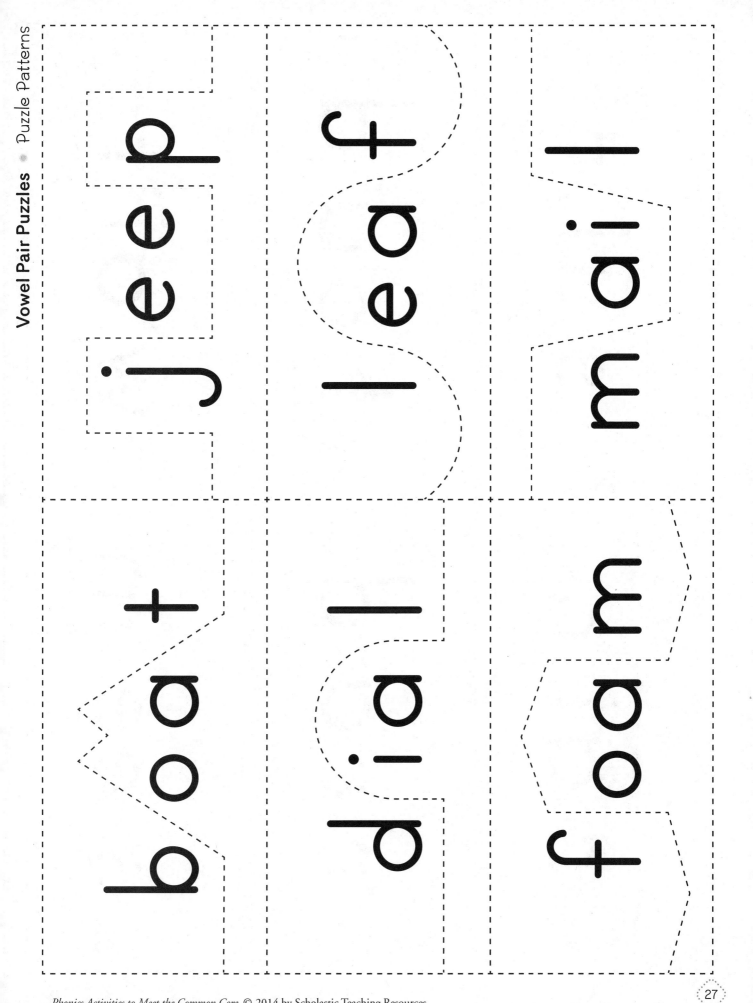

jeep

leaf

mail

boat

dial

foam

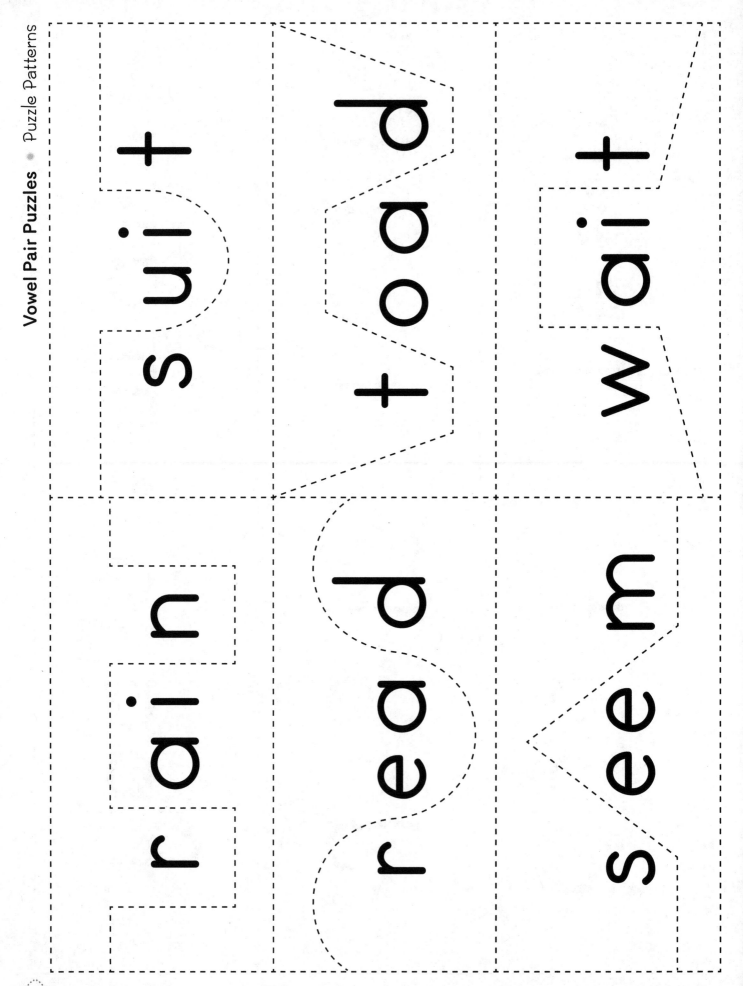

suit

toad

wait

rain

read

seem

Variant Vowel Pockets

This sorting activity provides children with a pocketful of fun learning about variant vowels.

Introduce the Concept

Display a book and a picture of the moon. Name each item, saying the word slowly and clearly. Ask children to listen for the different vowel sound in the words. Then show each of the picture cards with these vowel sounds. Name each picture and have children tell whether the vowel sound is like the one in *book* or *moon*. Next, show the *ou* and *ow* picture cards. Say each word and point out its spelling. Tell children that words with this vowel sound have two different spellings. Invite them to sort the picture cards by their word spellings. Repeat, using the *oi* and *oy* picture cards.

Preparing and Using the Activity

1. Color and cut out the pocket patterns and picture cards.

2. Fold the pocket cutouts up along the solid line and glue where indicated. (There will be a pocket below the picture on each side.)

3. To use, invite children choose a set of pockets and the corresponding picture cards.

4. Ask children to name the picture on each card, listening carefully to the vowel sound in the word and looking at its spelling. Then have them place the card in the pocket below the picture that has the same vowel sound and spelling.

Extend the Activity

Assemble the pocket pattern on page 33, then use the set of pockets and picture cards to reinforce the hard and soft sounds of *c* at the beginning of words. Also, you might use the pocket pattern as a template to make an additional set of pockets to reinforce the hard and soft sounds of *g*. Simply mask the words and pictures at the top of the pattern, add your own words and pictures (such as *gum* and *giraffe*), then copy, cut out, and assemble the pocket pattern. Use magazine cutouts, clip art, or your own drawings to make picture cards.

Materials

- pocket patterns and picture cards (pages 30–32)
- crayons
- scissors
- glue

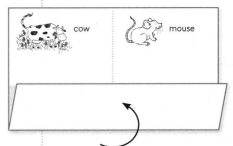

✦ ✦ ✦ **Tip** ✦ ✦ ✦

If you laminate the pockets, use a craft knife to cut the pockets open.

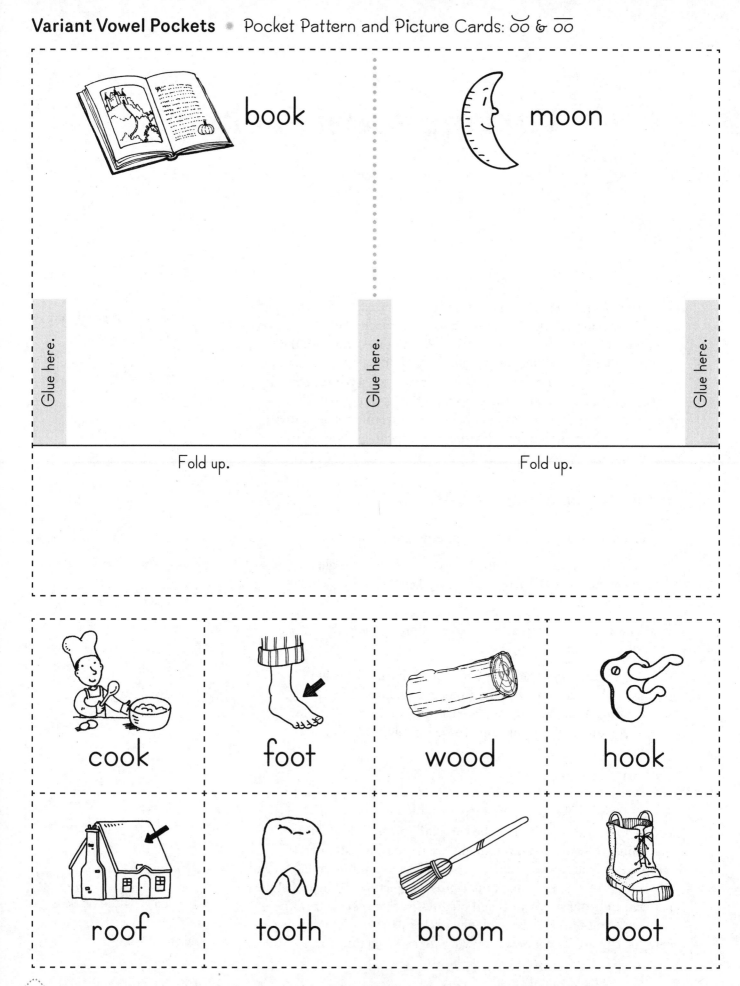

book

moon

Glue here.

Glue here.

Glue here.

Fold up.

Fold up.

cook

foot

wood

hook

roof

tooth

broom

boot

Phonics Activities to Meet the Common Core © 2014 by Scholastic Teaching Resources

cow

mouse

Glue here.

Glue here.

Glue here.

Fold up.

Fold up.

clown

gown

owl

plow

house

mouth

sprout

cloud

coin

boy

Glue here.

Glue here.

Glue here.

Fold up.

Fold up.

soil

boil

point

oil

toy

Soy Sauce

soy

joy

coy

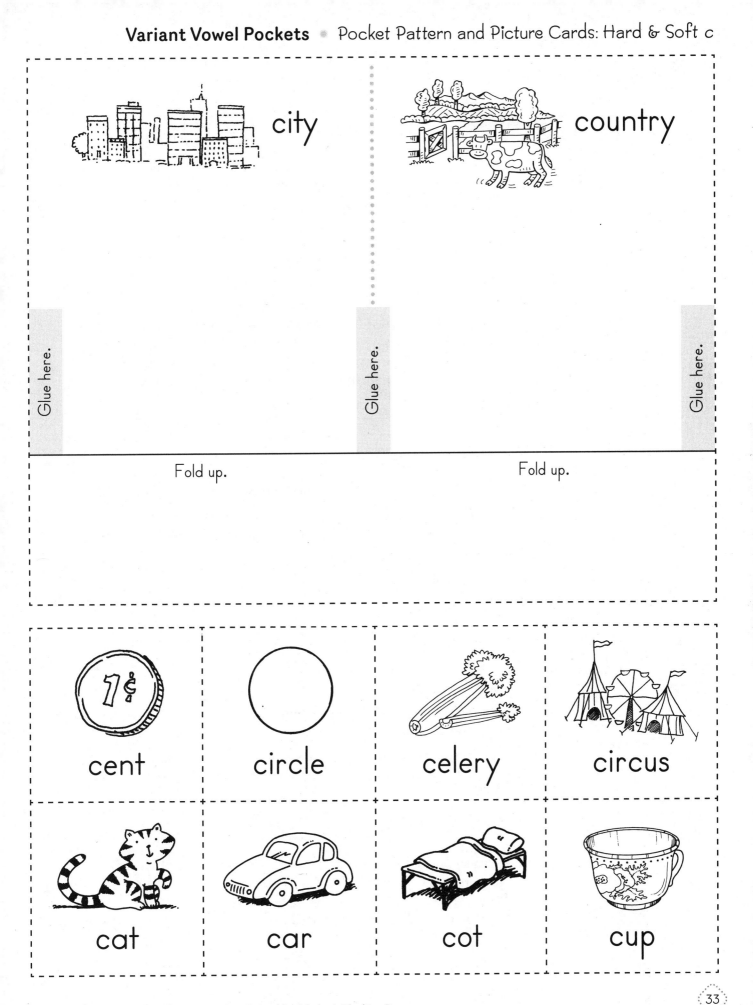

city

country

Glue here.

Glue here.

Glue here.

Fold up.

Fold up.

cent

circle

celery

circus

cat

car

cot

cup

R-Controlled Vowel Riddles

Use these fun riddles to add a touch of mystery to working with words that have *r*-controlled vowels.

Materials

- riddle cards (pages 35–36)
- picture cards (page 37)
- crayons
- scissors

Introduce the Concept

Show each picture card, read its name aloud, and have children repeat after you. Then point out the letter *r* in the word. Explain that this letter controls how the vowel or vowels in the word sounds. Next write each word on the board and invite a volunteer to circle the *r*-controlled vowel.

Preparing and Using the Activity

1. Color and cut out the riddle and picture cards.

2. To make the activity self-checking, match each card to its riddle. Then write the number for that riddle on the back of the card.

3. Laminate all of the pieces for durability.

4. To use, have children choose a riddle card. They then read each riddle and look for the picture card that fits the riddle.

5. Ask children to place each picture card on the box for its matching riddle.

6. Instruct children to check their answers on the back of the cards.

Extend the Activity

Challenge children to make up their own riddles for words such as *star, girl, purse, world, dirt,* and *work.* Invite them to read the riddles aloud for the class to solve.

✦ Tip ✦

Distribute copies of the riddles and word cards. Ask children to color, cut out, and glue each card to the corresponding riddle. Help them cut apart the riddles on each riddle card, stack the strips, and staple along the left side to make riddle books to share with others.

4

I move along the ground, but have no legs.

5

I'm big and furry. I live in the woods.

6

Feeling sick? I help you get well.

1

I stand on four legs. You can sit on me.

2

My feathers help me fly. Tweet! Tweet!

3

I am home to animals on a farm.

10	11	12
Blow air into me to make music!	I have one collar and two sleeves.	Wear me outside on a cold winter day.

7	8	9
You come to me to buy new things.	Small green leaves grow along my stems.	I live in the ocean. See my sharp teeth!

R-Controlled Vowel Riddles • Picture Cards

chair

bird

barn

worm

bear

nurse

store

fern

shark

horn

shirt

scarf

Consonant Blend Trains

Set children on track for learning about consonant blends
with these attachable trains.

Materials

- train engine (page 39), one for each consonant blend
- train car (page 39), four for each consonant blend
- consonant blend labels (page 40)
- picture cards (pages 40–41)
- crayons
- scissors
- Velcro dots

★ Tip ★

Copy the train engine and cars onto colorful construction paper. If desired, use the same color for the engine and cars that belong to the same consonant-blend group.

Introduce the Concept

Display one picture card that begins with each consonant blend in the activity. Then show children another picture card for each consonant blend. For each card, have children say the word and identify its beginning sound. Write that word on the board and invite a volunteer to circle the initial consonant blend. Finally, ask children to find the picture on display that begins with the same sound.

Preparing and Using the Activity

1. Cut out the train cars and consonant blend labels. Glue a label to each engine where indicated.

2. Color and cut out each picture card. For self-checking purposes, write the initial consonant blend on the back of the card.

3. Laminate the pieces for durability.

4. Attach the hook part of a Velcro dot to the back of the tab on the right side of the engine and each car. Affix the loop part to the front of the tab on the left side of each car.

5. Ask children to connect four cars at the Velcro dots. Then have them connect the train of cars to the engine of their choice.

6. Have children find the picture cards that go with the consonant blend on their engine. They check their answers on the back, then place the cards on the train cars.

Extend the Activity

Make additional consonant blend labels and picture cards, including two- and three-letter blends. You might also prepare the activity to teach and reinforce final consonant blends or initial and final consonant digraphs.

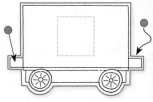

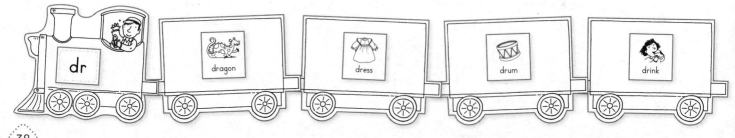

Phonics Activities to Meet the Common Core © 2014 by Scholastic Teaching Resources

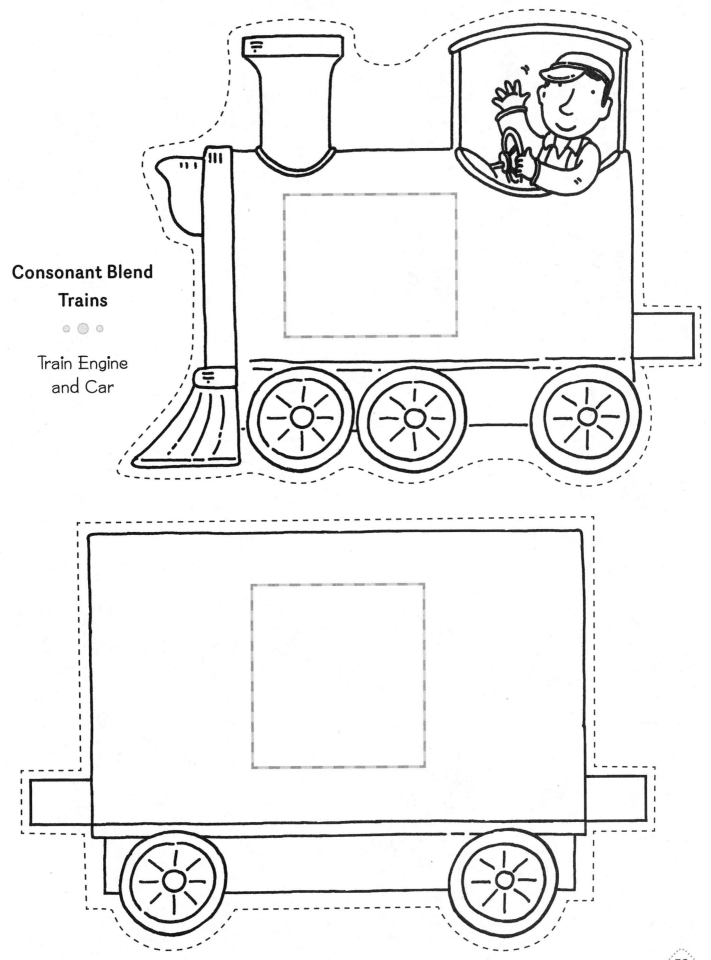

Consonant Blend Trains

Train Engine and Car

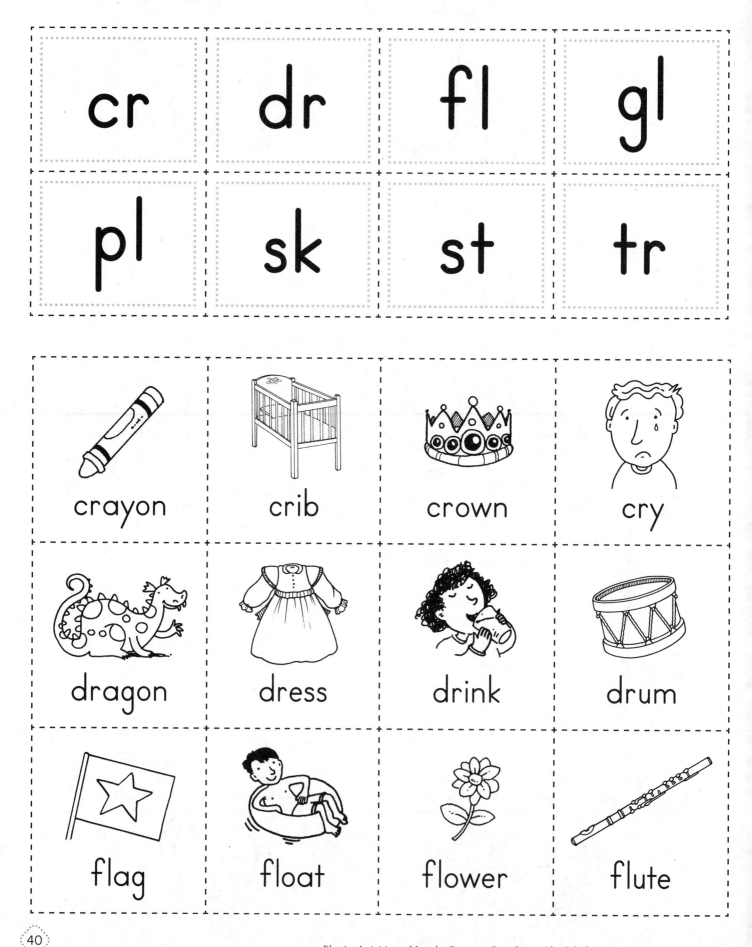

cr | dr | fl | gl

pl | sk | st | tr

crayon | crib | crown | cry

dragon | dress | drink | drum

flag | float | flower | flute

glass

globe

glove

glue

plate

plow

plug

plum

skate

ski

skirt

skunk

stamp

sticks

stop

stump

tray

tree

truck

trumpet

Digraph Sort & Slot

The slots in this easy-to-make rack provide children with a quick way
to sort and organize words that begin with consonant digraphs.

Materials

- tagboard digraph rack pattern (page 43)
- picture cards (page 44)
- scissors
- stapler
- crayons

★ ✦ **Tip** ✦ ★

If you laminate the rack, use
a craft knife to cut the slots
open.

Introduce the Concept

Display one picture card that begins with each consonant digraph in
the activity. Then show children another picture card for each digraph.
For each card, have children say the word and identify the sound at
the beginning of the word. Write that word on the board and invite a
volunteer to circle the initial digraph. Finally, ask children to find the
picture on display that begins with the same sound.

Preparing and Using the Activity

1. Cut out the rack pattern. Fold the cutout
   along the solid lines, as shown. Then
   staple the folded sections in place along
   the left and right edges. When finished,
   the rack will have three slots.

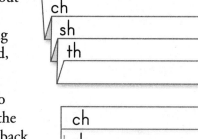

2. Color and cut out the picture cards. To
   make the activity self-checking, write the
   initial digraph for each picture on the back
   of that card.

3. To use, have children name the picture
   on each card and identify its beginning
   sound. They then identify the letter
   combination (or digraph) for that sound.

4. Ask children to place the card in the slot labeled with the matching
   consonant digraph.

5. Instruct children to check their answers on the back of the cards.

Extend the Activity

Challenge children to search print around the room to find words that
begin with the consonant digraphs *ch*, *sh*, and *th*. As children share their
findings, list their words on chart paper. Afterward, read aloud each word
with children. If desired, expand the list to include words that begin with
other digraphs, such as *wh* (*wheel*), *ph* (*phone*), and *thr* (*three*).

ch

sh

th

Digraph Sort & Slot • Picture Cards

*Phonics Activities to Meet
the Common Core*
© 2014 by Scholastic
Teaching Resources

Word Family Rhyme Boxes

Use these unique boxes to give children practice in grouping words that belong to the same word family.

Introduce the Concept

Write a few word-family endings (such as *-at, -ell,* and *-ide*) on the board. Review the pronunciation of each one. Then ask children to brainstorm words that end with each of these spellings. List their responses below each appropriate word-family ending. Explain that words that share a common spelling, such as the ones in your lists, make up a family of words. Can they think of other words that belong to the same word family? As children share, add the new word families they come up with to your lists on the board.

Preparing and Using the Activity

1. Cut out each rhyme box. Attach the hook part of a Velcro dot to each section on each rhyme box cutout.

2. To assemble each box, fold up the bottom section and glue at the right where indicated. Then fold back along each vertical line. Glue the right edge labeled with the dot over the short folded edge, matching the dots at the top. When finished, you'll have a stand-alone box with a pocket at the bottom of each side.

3. Cut out the word family labels. Attach the loop part of a Velcro dot to the back of each label.

4. Color and cut out each picture card. To make self-correcting, label the back of the card with the name of the picture.

5. To use, attach a word family label to each side of a box. Then have children name the pictures on the cards. Instruct them to put each card that belongs to a word family into the corresponding pocket on the box.

6. Have children check their answers on the back of the cards.

Extend the Activity

Give children practice with additional word families. Simply use the blank cards on pages 47 and 49 to make your own word family labels and picture cards to use with a word family rhyme box.

Materials

- 2 tagboard rhyme boxes (page 46)
- word family labels (page 47)
- picture cards (pages 47–49)
- scissors
- glue
- crayons
- Velcro dots

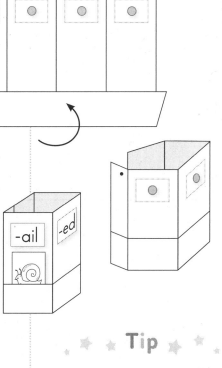

✦ ✦ Tip ✦ ✦

If you want to laminate the rhyme boxes, fold up the bottom tab, glue where indicated, then laminate. Use a craft knife to cut open the pockets, then add the Velcro and fold and assemble the box. (Use craft glue.)

Word Family Rhyme Boxes ● Box Pattern

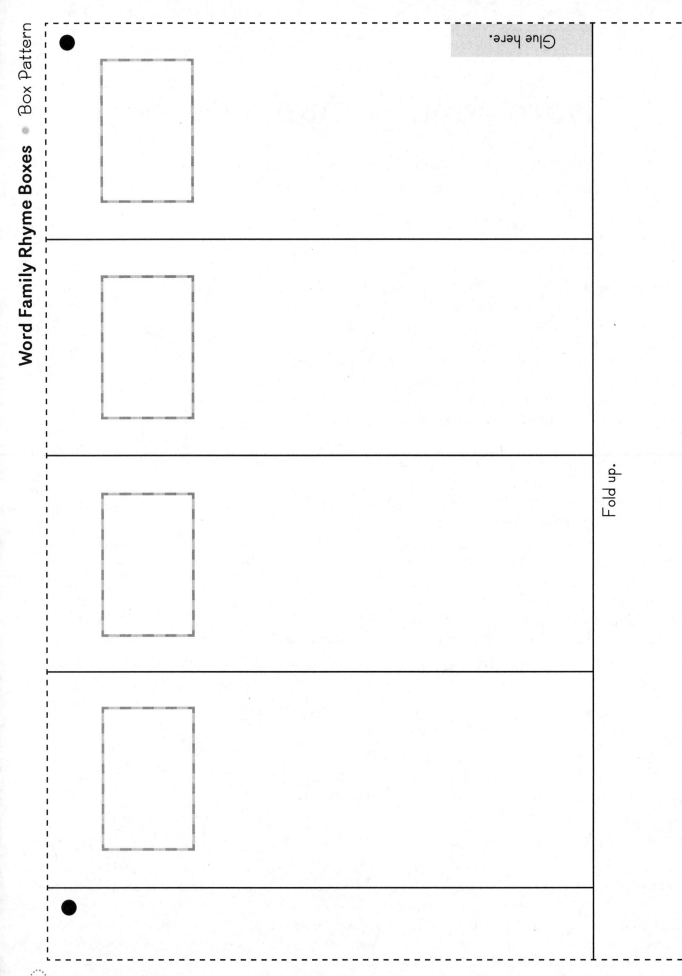

Glue here.

Fold up.

Glue here.

Word Family Rhyme Boxes • Word Family Labels and Picture Cards

-an	-ail	-ed	-eep
-ing	-ice	-ock	-oat
-ug	-unk		

Phonics Activities to Meet the Common Core © 2014 by Scholastic Teaching Resources

Word Family Rhyme Boxes  Picture Cards

Sight Word Sentence Cones

Children can dial words on these cones to make sentences
and practice their sight-word recognition.

Materials

- enlarged tagboard cone patterns (pages 51–52), each set copied on a different color
- scissors
- glue
- paper and pencil (for students)

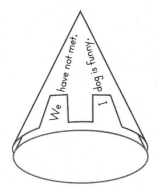

Introduce the Concept

Write these following sentence frames on the board: "_____ bird flew away." and "_____ book is red." In a box above the frames, write the words *The*, *A*, *My*, *We*, and *Come*. (Capitalize all of the words.) Read each sentence frame, then ask children to fill in the missing word using words from the box. As they try each word, ask if the sentence makes sense. If so, write the word on the line and read the sentence aloud with the class. Then erase the first word and continue. To wrap up, invite children to write one of the sentences, using the word of their choice in the blank, and then illustrate their sentence.

Preparing and Using the Activity

1. Cut out the patterns for Cone 1. (Cut along the center line to separate the patterns.)

2. To assemble each cone, overlap the straight edges, matching the symbols near the corners. Glue in place.

3. Nest the word cone into the notched cone with the sentence frames.

4. Repeat steps 1–3 to make Cone 2.

5. To use, have children choose Cone 1 or Cone 2. Instruct them to choose a word on the inner cone and then "dial" the outer cone until a sentence frame lines up with the word.

6. Have children read the sentence. Does it make sense? If so, they write the sentence on a sheet of paper.

7. After children have made as many sentences as possible with their cone, invite them to repeat the activity with the other cone.

Extend the Activity

Ask children to choose five of the sentences on their paper to illustrate. Then invite them to share their work with a partner. More advanced children can choose a sentence to use as a story starter.

Tip

Laminate the cutouts before you assemble the cones. (Use craft glue or clear tape to assemble.)

Sight Word Sentence Cones

Cone 1 Patterns

Word Cone

Sentence Frame Cone

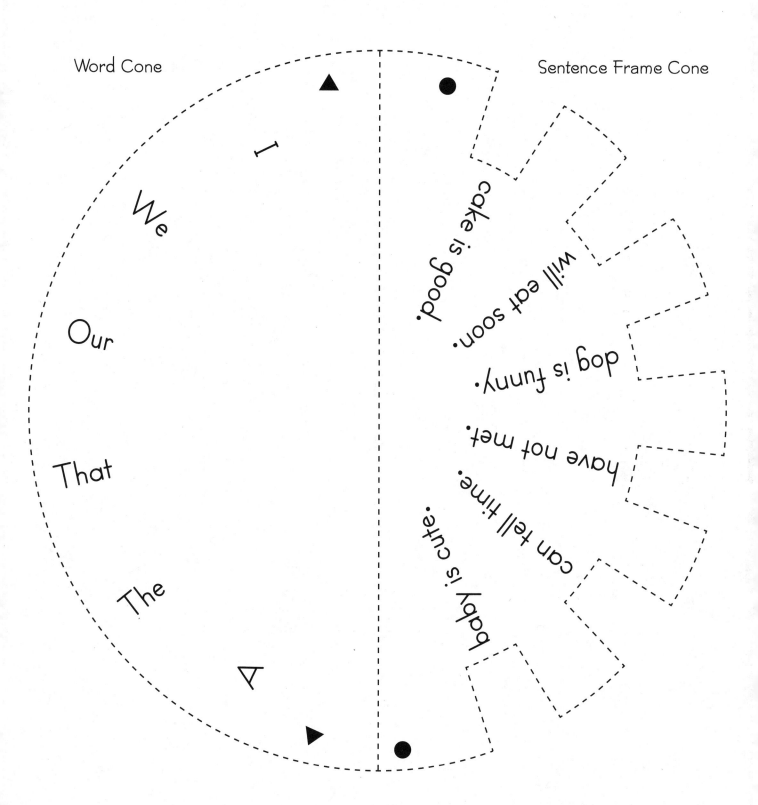

I

We

Our

That

The

A

cake is good.

will eat soon.

dog is funny.

have not met.

can tell time.

baby is cute.

Sight Word Sentence Cones

Cone 2 Patterns

Word Cone

Sentence Frame Cone

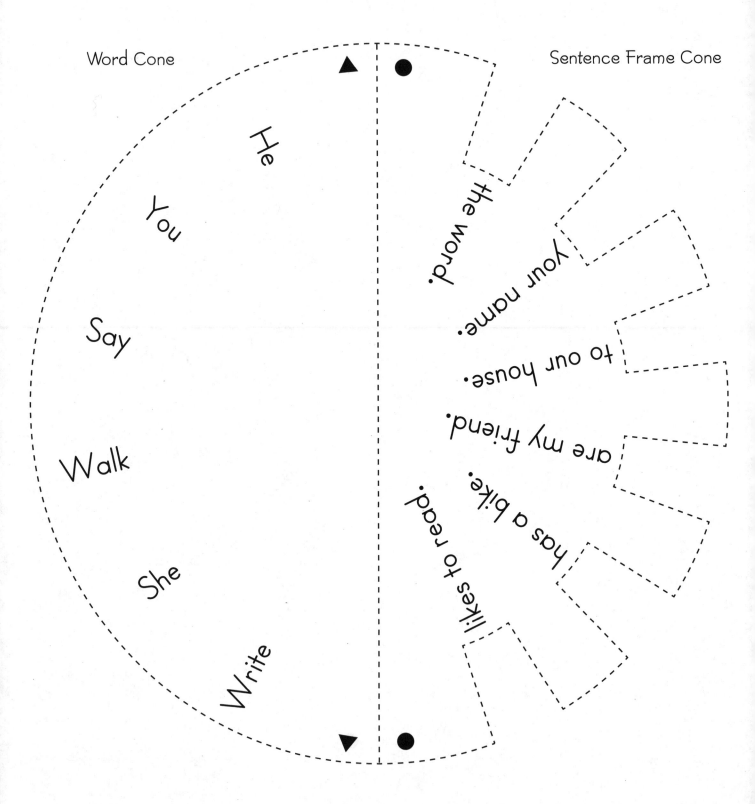

He

You

Say

Walk

She

Write

the word.

your name.

to our house.

are my friend.

has a bike.

likes to read.

Egg-Basket Word Categories

A-tisket, a-tasket, in this activity, children sort color and number words
into the proper basket!

Introduce the Concept

Hold up a color or number card. Read the word and have children
repeat it aloud. Then ask if the word is a color or number word.
Display the color words together on one side of the board and the
number words on the other side. After children are familiar
with the words, have them match the word cards to the actual
colors and numbers.

Preparing and Using the Activity

1. Color and cut out the baskets.

2. Cut out the basket labels and word cards. Glue a
   label to each basket.

3. Laminate the baskets and cards for durability.

4. To use, have children read the word on each card.

5. If the word names a color, children put that card on
   the "Colors" basket. If the word names a number,
   they put the card on the "Numbers" basket.

Extend the Activity

Further reinforce children's recognition of color and
number words with this idea. First, have them write
each word on a sheet of paper. Then ask them to draw a color
patch beside each color word, using a crayon in that color. Have
them write the corresponding numeral next to each number word.
Additionally, you might have children write and illustrate sentences
using the color and number words from the activity.

Materials

- 2 construction-paper
  baskets (page 54)
- basket labels and word
  cards (page 55)
- crayons
- scissors
- glue

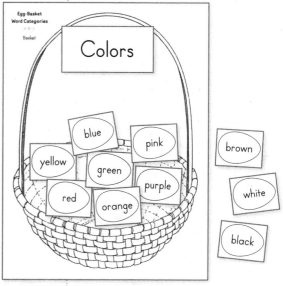

✦ ✦ Tip ✦ ✦

To add a self-checking feature,
put a dot of the matching
color on the back of each
color card and write the
corresponding numeral on the
back of each number card.

Egg-Basket
Word Categories

Basket

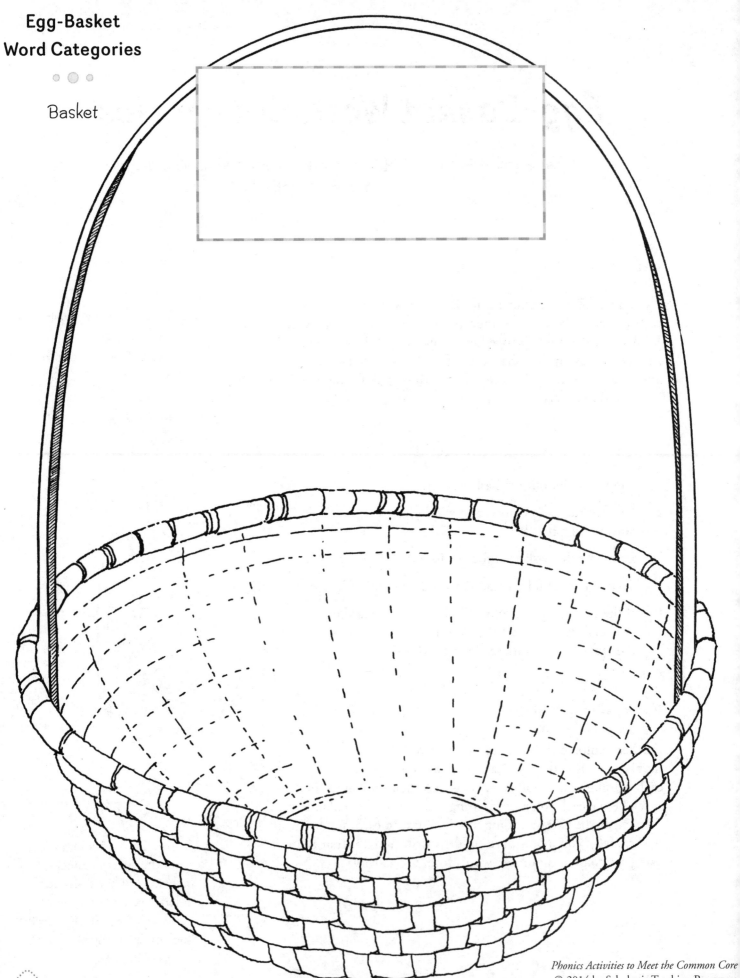

Phonics Activities to Meet the Common Core
© 2014 by Scholastic Teaching Resources

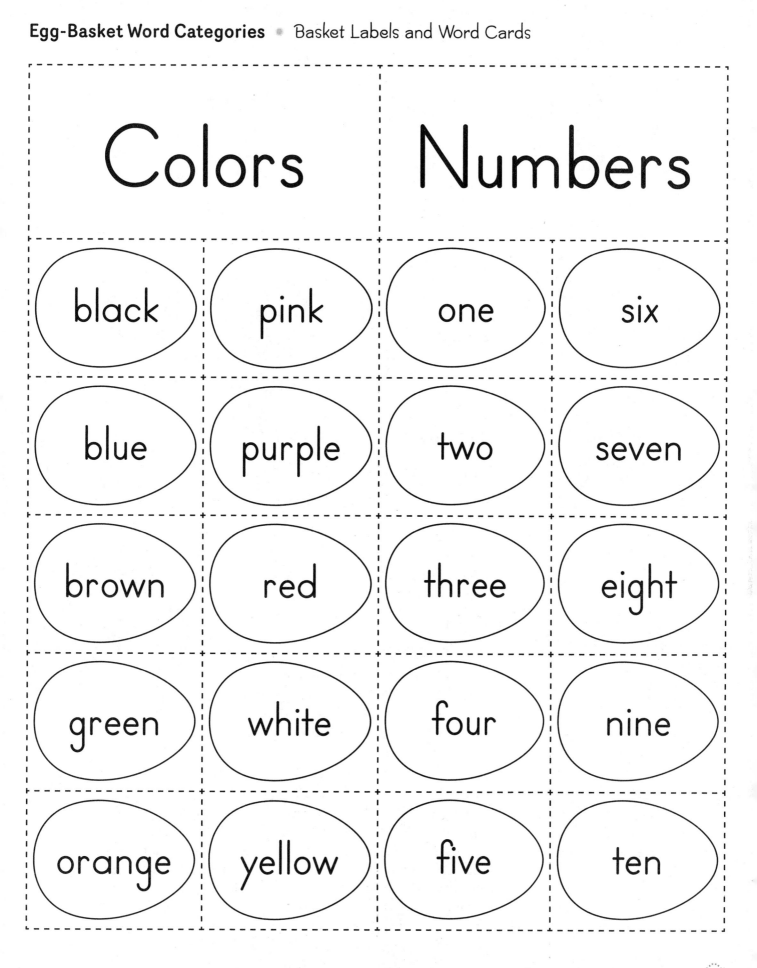

Colors

Numbers

black	pink	one	six
blue	purple	two	seven
brown	red	three	eight
green	white	four	nine
orange	yellow	five	ten

Compound-Word Wheels

With this big wheel, children match up words to create a number of compound words.

Materials

- large and small tagboard wheels (pages 57–58)
- scissors
- paper fastener
- paper and pencil (for students)

Introduce the Concept

Tell children that when two words are put together, they make a new word called a *compound word*. Name some compound words, such as *butterfly*, *baseball*, and *raincoat*. Write each example on the board, then separate the word into its two smaller words. Afterward, invite children to brainstorm additional compound words. Help them break each word apart into the two words that it is composed of.

Preparing and Using the Activity

1. Cut out the large and small wheels.

2. Use the paper fastener to attach the small wheel to the large one.

3. Review the words on each wheel.

4. To use, have children choose a word on the large wheel. Ask them to read the word and then turn the small wheel, lining up each word with their word. Do the two words together make a compound word?

5. If children make a compound word, have them write it on a sheet of paper. Encourage them to make as many compound words as they can.

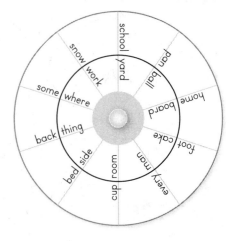

Extend the Activity

Play this game to help build children's vocabulary. First, choose a compound word that can be made on the word wheel. (Keep it a secret!) Then make up clues or give hints to children about the word to help them guess the mystery word. For instance, for *football*, you might tell children that the mystery word is used in a game, it can be found on a large field, and it is usually brown. Invite children to use the word wheel to help them discover the mystery word.

✦ ✦ Tip ✦ ✦

Laminate the wheels before you assemble them with the paper fastener.

Compound-Word Wheels

Large Wheel

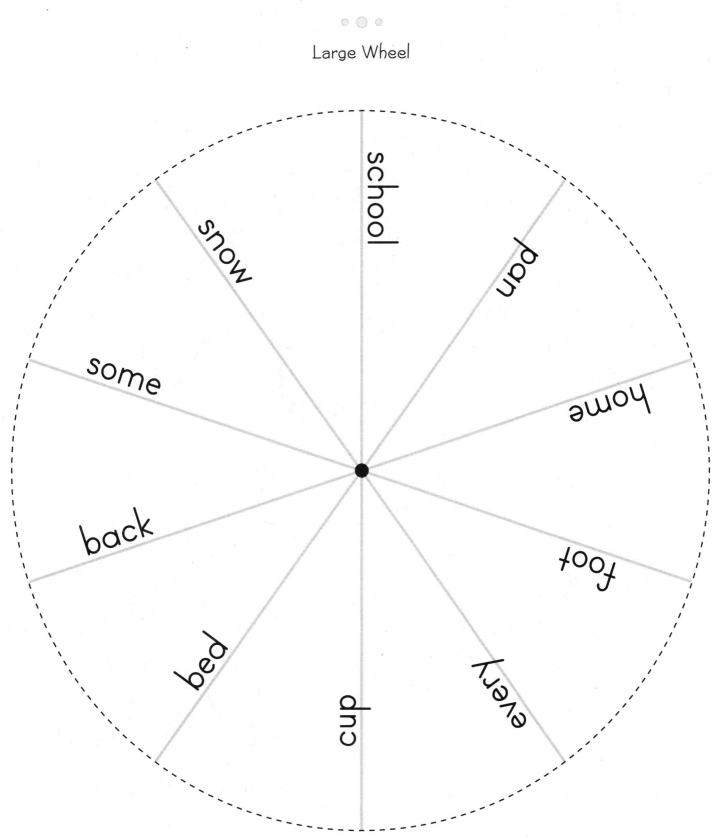

Compound-Word Wheels

Small Wheel

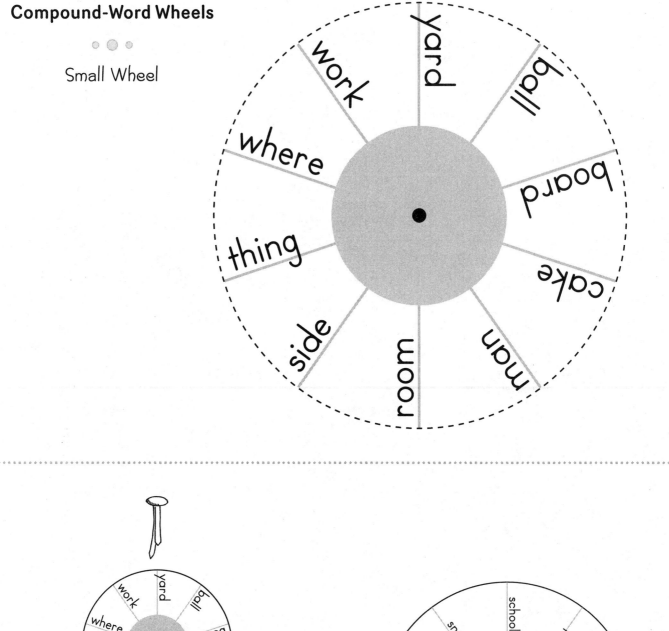

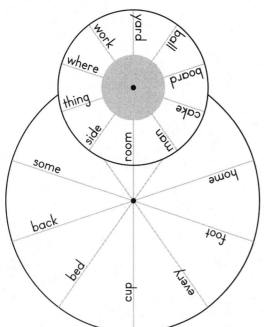

Reading Into Feelings

Children match emotions to text with this simple comprehension activity.

Introduce the Concept

Show each emotion card to children. Read the word aloud and have children repeat it. Then invite volunteers to share about situations in which they have experienced that emotion. Finally, make up situations that might elicit one of the emotions featured on the cards. After describing the situation, ask children to find the card that best depicts the emotion one would experience in that situation.

Preparing and Using the Activity

1. Color and cut out the emotion cards.

2. To make the activity self-checking, write the following numbers on the back of the emotion cards: *1* on *happy*, *2* on *tired*, *3* on *surprised*, *4* on *grumpy*, *5* on *sad*, and *6* on *afraid*.

3. Laminate the text page and emotion cards.

4. To use, have children read each section on the text page. How might they feel in that situation?

5. Ask children to find the emotion card that matches their feeling. They then place it on the text page in the corresponding section.

6. Instruct children to check their answers on the back of the cards.

Extend the Activity

Distribute half-sheets of paper and copies of the emotion cards. Ask children to color and cut out the cards. Then have them glue each card on a separate sheet of paper and write a sentence or two about a situation that elicits that feeling. When finished, children can stack their pages behind a cover and staple them together to create a book about emotions.

Materials

- text page (page 60)
- one set of emotion cards (page 61)
- crayons
- scissors

✦ ✦ **Tip** ✦ ✦

Children can use the extra sets of emotion cards (page 61) for "Extend the Activity."

I dropped my books.
I spilled my milk.
I'm having a bad day.
How do I feel?

My dog ran away.
I miss him.
I'm not happy.
How do I feel?

I saw a big snake.
I ran inside.
How do I feel?

I'm going to ride
my new bike today!
How do I feel?

I worked so hard!
I need a nap.
How do I feel?

I go into a room
and my friends call out,
"Happy Birthday!"
How do I feel?

Syllable Trees

This syllable-tree activity will help children grow to understand
that words can have one or more syllables.

Materials

- 3 syllable trees (page 63)
- picture cards (page 64)
- crayons
- scissors
- marker

Introduce the Concept

Display several picture cards in which the picture names have one, two,
or three syllables. Point to one card at a time and name the picture.
Repeat the name, this time clapping as you say each syllable. Ask
children to count the number of times you clap. Tell them that this is
the number of syllables in the word. Finally, invite children to say the
word with you while clapping out the syllables.

Preparing and Using the Activity

1. Color and cut out the picture cards
   and three syllable trees.

2. Write 1, 2, or 3 on the line on each
   tree trunk.

3. To make the activity self-checking,
   label the back of each picture card
   with the number of syllables in that
   word.

4. Laminate the pieces for durability.

5. Review the picture on each card with
   children.

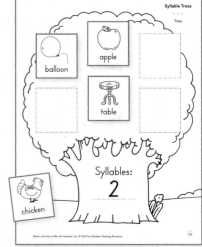

6. To use, have children name the
   picture on each card and count the syllables in its name. They
   then place the card on the corresponding tree.

7. Instruct children to check their answers on the back of the cards.

Extend the Activity

Create additional picture cards to use with the activity. If desired,
prepare a tree and make cards for words that have four syllables. To
further explore syllabication, invite children to write their names on a
card and use these cards in the activity. You might also have them make
cards picturing common items around the classroom for the activity.

Tip

You might make copies of
the trees and picture cards
for children's use. Have
children label each tree
with a number (for syllable
count) and then glue
each picture card to the
corresponding tree. They
can take their trees home
to share what they know
about syllabication.

Syllables:

_____

car

dog

hand

house

shoe

zoo

apple

balloon

chicken

table

wagon

zipper

banana

dinosaur

hamburger

newspaper

triangle

umbrella